Exploring Southeast Asia with Chuah Thean Teng:
Father of Batik Painting

Eva Wong Nava is an award-winning children's book author. She writes picture books to entertain, engage, and enthral young readers. She is also an art historian. When not writing for children, she meanders art museums and galleries waiting for the next piece of art work to speak to her and inspire another story. She weaves stories from art at *CarpeArte* Journal. When not writing, Eva teaches the art of picture book creation through her workshops under the brand, Picture Book Matters. Eva can be found on Twitter, Instagram and Facebook engaging people in conversations about art and stories.

Jeffrey Say is an art historian specialising in Singapore and Southeast Asian art history. Jeffrey has been instrumental in the development of art history studies at LASALLE College of the Arts, supporting artists to develop a contextual and historical understanding of the evolution of visual arts. In 2009, he designed the world's first Master's programme focussing on Asian modern and contemporary art histories. Jeffrey is a public advocate of the importance of art history to Singapore. He is a frequent public speaker at museums, universities and galleries, and conducts short courses which remain hugely popular among various publics. Jeffrey is also a regular commentator on the local visual arts scene. An author of numerous essays on art, his seminal co-edited work *Histories, Practices, Interventions: A Reader in Singapore Contemporary Art* (2016) remains a critical anthology for researchers, curators and students on Singapore art to date.

Quek Hong Shin is a Singaporean freelance author and illustrator whose works include picture books like *The Amazing Sarong, The Brilliant Oil Lamp and Universe of Feelings. The Incredible Basket*, was the winner of Best Children's Book at the 2019 Singapore Book Awards. He is also the illustrator for other children's titles like *The One and Only Inuka and the Ahoy, Navy*! series that was published in celebration of the Republic of Singapore Navy's 50th Anniversary in 2017.

PENGUIN BOOKS

USA | Canada | UK | Ireland | Australia
New Zealand | India | South Africa | China | Southeast Asia

Penguin Books is part of the Penguin Random House group
of companies whose addresses can be found at global.
penguinrandomhouse.com

Published by Penguin Random House SEA Pte Ltd
9, Changi South Street 3, Level 08-01,
Singapore 486361

Penguin
Random House
SEA

First published in Penguin Books by Penguin Random House
SEA 2022

ISBN 9789814954372

www.penguin.sg

EXPLORING SOUTHEAST ASIA WITH

CHUAH THEAN TENG

FATHER OF BATIK PAINTING

Eva Wong Nava and Jeffrey Say

Illustrated by Quek Hong Shin

PENGUIN BOOKS

An imprint of Penguin Random House

Teng scanned the cavernous room he was standing in.

Remnants of fabric were scattered across the floor. Teng's ears picked up the faint whirring and ticking the machines around him were making.

These familiar sounds made him happy.

Soon, they hummed to a stop, and silence filled the space. Teng's heart pulled. He knew this would be the last time his factory would be printing batik.

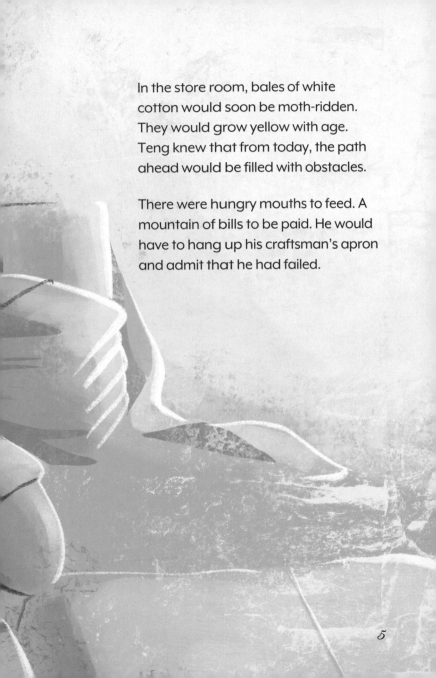

In the store room, bales of white cotton would soon be moth-ridden. They would grow yellow with age. Teng knew that from today, the path ahead would be filled with obstacles.

There were hungry mouths to feed. A mountain of bills to be paid. He would have to hang up his craftsman's apron and admit that he had failed.

This wasn't the first time that Teng had endured challenges. The worst of the war years was over. He had felt hunger, heartache, and fear when Malaya was under occupation. What could be worse than fearing for your life every day for almost four years?

6

But, his children, wife, and family—
they were all Teng could think of as
the factory gate clinked behind him.

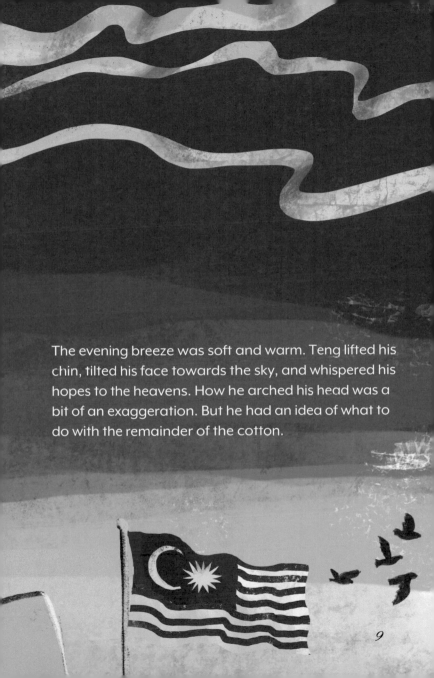

The evening breeze was soft and warm. Teng lifted his chin, tilted his face towards the sky, and whispered his hopes to the heavens. How he arched his head was a bit of an exaggeration. But he had an idea of what to do with the remainder of the cotton.

I am an artist and here
is a medium I can work with.
I was trained by the best
masters in China.
I know about painting.
I am a craftsman,
trained in making batik.

'Why can't I do both?' he said to himself.

Teng's heart raced in excitement.
His head churned with ideas.
The West shall meet the East.

I will meet them in the middle.

Teng set to work immediately.

Teng walked back and forth in his tiny studio.
Thinking, thinking, thinking.

I can paint people, animals, and the kampung. I will paint from memory and document the people and land of Malaysia. I will use the technique of batik-printing to make art, and people will hang my paintings on their walls.

Teng's heart thudded with emotion.

It was a hot day, but a slight breeze was blowing. It fluttered in through an open window, carrying nature's moods with it. Teng looked outside, and his vision filled with the swirling colours of his home.

'There is grace and beauty all around,' he said. His heart thumped against his chest. He must put all this gorgeousness down immediately.

I know life is short
and there is
not a moment
to spare.

Day in and day out, Teng went to work.
He combined Western painting and batik-crafting.
Many weeks and several months dragged by.
Six months in, he was pulling his hair in frustration.
Twelve months after, he started to pace his studio
in desperation.

16

And, two years later, he had lost his inspiration. Nothing he did could translate these ideas churning in his head into images. The colours simply would not stay on the canvas.

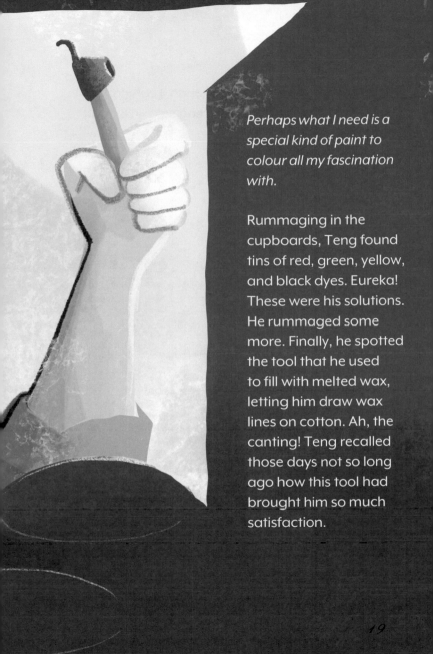

Perhaps what I need is a special kind of paint to colour all my fascination with.

Rummaging in the cupboards, Teng found tins of red, green, yellow, and black dyes. Eureka! These were his solutions. He rummaged some more. Finally, he spotted the tool that he used to fill with melted wax, letting him draw wax lines on cotton. Ah, the canting! Teng recalled those days not so long ago how this tool had brought him so much satisfaction.

19

'As a batik craftsman, I can do good work ...,' Teng said, inspired.

20

A loud whoop rang in the air.
But this time, it was not one of
frustration or desperation.

21

Soon Teng's studio became a hive of activities. He stretched the cotton across a wooden frame. Ah! Teng saw that he now had a canvas.

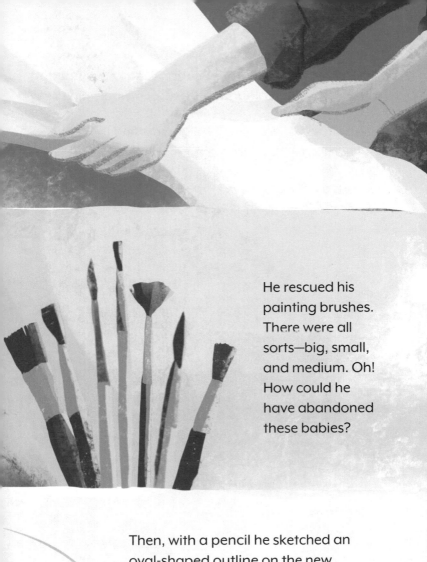

He rescued his painting brushes. There were all sorts—big, small, and medium. Oh! How could he have abandoned these babies?

Then, with a pencil he sketched an oval-shaped outline on the new canvas. Drip! Went the melted wax on the stretched white cotton.

From the French artist Georges Seurat, Teng knew that dots and dots and dots of colours could make a whole picture.

After many hours of dabbing here and dotting there, the canvas was filled with a familiar face.

Teng stepped back and took in the image of himself.

'If I can do this in batik, I could do anything,' he said. Teng wiped the tears from his eyes because after two years, he finally did it. He had completed a self-portrait by meeting east and west in the middle.

Who was Chuah Thean Teng?

Chuah Thean Teng (1914–2008) was born in Fukien, China. He was also known as Teng, the name he signed his artworks with. When he was eighteen years old, Chuah emigrated with his parents to Penang, Malaysia. When Chuah grew older, he returned to China to study art at the Xiamen Academy of Fine Art (also known as the Amoy Art Institute). He eventually returned to Malaysia. During the Second World War, Chuah moved to Indonesia to work at his uncle's batik factory, where he learned the craft of batik printing. Chuah returned to Penang and opened his own factory producing batik but it eventually closed down. He soon found a way to use the dye-pigments, wax, and bales of cotton to produce artworks filled with figures, motifs, and colours of his homeland, Malaysia. Chuah's works are known for their textures, which he created by layering the canvas with lines. He is remembered most for his depiction of women and children at play, rest, and work. Chuah is known as the 'Father of Batik Painting' since he was the pioneer in using batik as a medium for painting. He helped people to see that batik printing is more than a craft; it can also be a medium of art. His works are collected by major galleries and private collectors around the world. Chuah also greatly influenced whole generations of batik artists.

Chuah Thean Teng
Lullaby
Undated
Batik
85.5 x 87.5 cm
Collection of National Gallery Singapore

Chuah Thean Teng, or Teng, created this artwork but he did not date it. Artists often leave out the date of their creations. Sometimes they do this because they really cannot remember when they made the work of art, because an artwork can take months or years to finish. At times, they may simply have forgotten to date their works.